D1315237

Creatures of the Night

Hedgehogs
in the Dark

By Therese Harasymiw

 **Gareth Stevens**
Publishing

Please visit our website, www.garethstevens.com. For a free color catalog of all our high-quality books, call toll free 1-800-542-2595 or fax 1-877-542-2596.

Library of Congress Cataloging-in-Publication Data

Harasymiw, Therese.
Hedgehogs in the dark / Therese Harasymiw.
    p. cm. — (Creatures of the night)
Includes bibliographical references and index.
ISBN 978-1-4339-6374-2 (pbk.)
ISBN 978-1-4339-6375-9 (6-pack)
ISBN 978-1-4339-6372-8 (library binding)
1. Hedgehogs—Juvenile literature. 2. Nocturnal animals—Juvenile literature. I. Title.
QL737.E753H37 2012
599.33'2—dc23
                                    2011029957

First Edition

Published in 2013 by
Gareth Stevens Publishing
111 East 14th Street, Suite 349
New York, NY 10003

Copyright © 2013 Gareth Stevens Publishing

Designer: Daniel Hosek
Editor: Therese Shea

Photo credits: Cover, p. 1 Berndt Fischer/Oxford Scientific/Getty Images; pp. 5, 11, 13, 17, 21 Shutterstock.com; pp. 7, 9, 15 iStockphoto/Thinkstock.com; p. 19 Universal Images Group/ Getty Images.

Printed in the United States of America

CPSIA compliance information: Batch #CW12GS: For further information contact Gareth Stevens, New York, New York at 1-800-542-2595.

Contents

Small, Cute, and Prickly 4

Stop and Roll 10

Dinnertime 12

Hedgehogs Spit! 16

Hedgehog Babies 18

All in the Name 20

Glossary 22

For More Information 23

Index 24

Boldface words appear in the glossary.

Small, Cute, and Prickly

Hedgehogs may look cute, but you don't want to hug one! These animals have sharp **spines**. The spines help hedgehogs **protect** themselves. You probably won't see a hedgehog in the wild. They're mostly found in Africa, Asia, and Europe.

5

A hedgehog's body is usually no more than 1 foot (30 cm) long. Its tail is no more than 2 inches (5 cm) long. Its round body is covered with spines. However, it has fur on its legs, face, and belly.

Hedgehogs live in many kinds of places. Some live in hot deserts, while others live in cool forests. They're good swimmers. They can also climb trees. If hedgehogs fall, their many spines keep them from getting hurt!

Stop and Roll

When a hedgehog thinks it's in danger, it rolls into a ball. Its belly, head, and legs are hidden. Only its spines are sticking out. Most **predators**, such as foxes, see the spines and look for a meal that's easier to eat!

Dinnertime

Hedgehogs sleep curled up. Even if something **sneaks** up on them, they're protected. They sleep all day and wake up as the sun sets. They're night hunters. Hedgehogs mostly eat bugs and worms. They eat some small animals, too.

Hedgehogs eat **poisonous** snakes! How can they do this? When a snake bites, its teeth can't get through the hedgehog's spines to its skin. Some people think hedgehogs aren't affected by eating harmful plants, either.

Hedgehogs Spit!

Did you know hedgehogs spit on themselves? They cover their spines with spit. People have many ideas about why they do this. Some think it's a way to draw a **mate**. Others think it's to make themselves even less tasty to predators.

17

Hedgehog Babies

Hedgehog mothers have up to seven babies at a time. The babies are born with soft spines. After about 3 weeks, the soft spines become sharp and stiff. The babies leave their nest and look for food with their mother.

All in the Name

Hedgehogs got the "hog" part of their name because they grunt like pigs as they look for food. They make other noises, too. They scream when they're in danger. Their spines may stand up. These little animals can take care of themselves!

The Hedgehog Fact Box

Length	5 to 12 inches (13 to 30 cm)
Weight	up to 2 pounds (0.9 kg)
Where They Live	mostly in Europe, Asia, Africa
Life Span	about 7 years in the wild

Glossary

mate: one of two animals that come together to make babies

poisonous: having poison, which is something that causes illness or death

predator: an animal that hunts other animals for food

protect: to guard

sneak: to move or act in a secret way

spine: the sharp, stiff points on the body of an animal

For More Information

Books

Leach, Michael. *Hedgehog*. New York, NY: PowerKids Press, 2009.

Mulder, Nancy. *Caring for Your Hedgehog*. New York, NY: Weigl Publishers, 2007.

Websites

Hedgehog
www.awf.org/content/wildlife/detail/hedgehog
Find out more about hedgehogs and where they live.

Hedgehog
animals.howstuffworks.com/mammals/hedgehog-info.htm
Read how hedgehogs "talk" to each other.

Hedgehogs
kids.nationalgeographic.com/kids/animals/creaturefeature/hedgehog/
See lots of photos of hedgehogs as well as video.

Index

Africa 4, 21

Asia 4, 21

babies 18

belly 6, 10

body 6

bugs 12

deserts 8

Europe 4, 21

face 6

forests 8

fur 6

head 10

legs 6, 10

mate 16

noises 20

predators 10, 16

protect 4, 12

small animals 12

snakes 14

spines 4, 6, 8, 10, 14, 16, 18, 20

spit 16

worms 12